teacher's friend publications

September

a creative idea book for the elementary teacher

written and illustrated
by
Karen Sevaly

Copyright © 1989
Teacher's Friend Publications, Inc.
All rights reserved
Printed in the United States of America
Published by Teacher's Friend Publications, Inc.
7407 Orangewood Drive, Riverside, CA 92504

ISBN-0-943263-00-X

This book is dedicated to the teachers and staff of the Jurupa Unified School District. Their enthusiasm and earnest desire to motivate children has been a great inspiration.

I am most grateful for the encouragement of my husband, Richard Sevaly, and our two sons, James and Robert.

Table of Contents

WHAT IS IN
THIS BOOK:

You will find the following in each monthly idea book from Teacher's Friend Publications:

1. A calendar listing every day of the month with a classroom idea.

2. At least four new student awards to be sent home to parents.

3. Three new bookmarks that can be used in your school library or given to students by you as "Super Student Awards."

4. Numerous bulletin board ideas and patterns pertaining to the particular month.

5. Easy to make craft ideas related to the monthly holidays.

6. Dozens of activities emphasizing not only the obvious holidays but also the often forgotten anniversaries, such as; Mexican Independence Day, American Indian Day and the birthday of Johnny Appleseed.

7. Crossword puzzles, word finds, creative writing pages, booklet covers, bingo cards and much more.

8. Scores of classroom management techniques, the newest and the best.

HOW TO USE
THIS BOOK:

Every page of this book may be duplicated for individual classroom use.

Some pages are meant to be used as duplicating masters and used as student work sheets. Other pages may be copied onto construction paper or used as it is.

If you have access to a print shop, you will find that many pages work well when printed on index paper. This type of paper takes crayons and felt markers well and is sturdy enough to last and last. The visor pattern and bookmarks are two items that work particularly well on index paper.

Lastly, some pages are meant to be enlarged with an overhead or opaque projector. When we say enlarge, we mean it! Think BIG! Three, four or even five feet is great! Try using colored butcher paper or poster board so you don't spend all your time coloring.

Making the Most of It!

ADDING THE COLOR:

Putting the color to finished items can be a real bother to teachers in a rush. Try these ideas:

1. On small areas, water color markers work great. If your area is rather large switch to crayons or even colored chalk or pastels.

   (Don't worry, lamination or a spray fixative will keep the color on the work and off of you. No laminator or fixative? That's okay, a little hair spray will do the trick.)

2. The quickest method of coloring large items is to simply start with colored paper. (Poster board, butcher paper or large construction paper work well.) Add a few dashes of a contrasting colored marker or crayon and you will have it made.

3. Try cutting character eyes, teeth, etc. from white typing paper and gluing them in place. These features will really stand out and make your bulletin boards come alive.

   For special effects add real buttons or lace. Metallic paper looks great on stars and belt buckles, too.

LAMINATORS:

If you have access to a roll laminator you already know how fortunate you are. They are priceless when it comes to saving time and money. Try these ideas:

1. You can laminate more than just classroom posters and construction paper. Try various kinds of fabric, wall paper and gift wrapping. You'll be surprised at the great combinations you come up with.

   Laminated classified ads can be used to cut headings for current event bulletin boards. Colorful gingham fabric makes terrific cut letters or scalloped edging. You might even try burlap! It looks terrific on a fall bulletin board.

   (You can even make professional looking bookmarks with laminated fabric or burlap. They are great gift ideas.)

2. Felt markers and laminated paper or fabric can work as a team. Just make sure the markers you use are permanent and not water based. Oops, make a mistake! That's okay. Put a little ditto fluid on a tissue, rub across the mark and presto, it's gone! (Dry transfer markers work great on lamination, too.

Making the Most of It!

LAMINATORS:
(continued)

3. Laminating cut-out characters can be tricky. If you have enlarged an illustration onto poster board, simply laminate first and then cut it out with an art knife. (Just make sure the laminator is plenty hot.)

One problem may arise when you paste an illustration onto poster board and laminate the finished product. If your paste-up does not cover 100% of the illustration, the poster board may separate from it after laminating. To avoid this problem, paste your illustration onto poster board that measures slightly larger. This way, the lamination will help hold down your illustration.

4. Have you ever laminated student made place mats, crayon shavings, tissue paper collages, or dried flowers? You'll be amazed at the variety of creative things that can be laminated and used in the classroom, or as take-home gifts.

DITTO MASTERS:

Many of the pages in this book can be made into masters for duplicating. Try some of these ideas for best results:

1. When using new masters, turn down the pressure on the duplicating machine. As the copies become light, increase the pressure. This will get longer wear out of both the master and the machine.

2. If the print from the back side of your original comes through the front when making a master or photocopy, slip a sheet of black construction paper behind the sheet. This will mask the unwanted black lines and create a much better copy.

3. Trying to squeeze one more run out of that worn master can be frustrating. Try lightly spraying the inked side of the master with hair spray. For some reason, this helps the master put out those few extra copies.

4. Several potential masters in this book contain instructions for the teacher. Simply cover the type with correction fluid or a small slip of paper before duplicating.

Making the Most of It!

BULLETIN BOARD
BACKGROUNDS

Creating clever bulletin boards for your classroom need not take fantastic amounts of time and money. With a little preparation and know-how you can have different boards each month with very little effort. Try some of these ideas:

1. Background paper should be put up only once a year. Choose colors that can go with many themes and holidays. A black butcher paper background will look terrific with springtime butterflies or a spooky Halloween display.

2. Butcher paper is not the only thing that can be used to cover the back of your board. You might like to try the classified ad section of the local newspaper for a current events board. Or how about colored burlap? Just fold it up at the end of the year to reuse again.

   Wallpaper is another great background cover. Discontinued rolls can be purchased for next to nothing at discount hardware stores. Most can be wiped clean and will not fade like construction paper. (Do not glue wall paper directly to the board, just staple or pin in place.)

ON-GOING
BULLETIN BOARDS

Creating the on-going bulletin board can be easy. Give one of these ideas a try.

1. Choose one board to be a calendar display. Students can change this monthly. They can do the switching of dates, month titles and holiday symbols. Start the year with a great calendar board and with a few minor changes each month it will add a sparkle to the classroom.

2. A classroom tree bulletin board is another one that requires very little attention after September. Cut a large bare tree from brown butcher paper and display it in the center of the board. (Wood-grained adhesive paper makes a great tree, also.) Children can add fall leaves, flowers, apples, Christmas ornaments, birds, valentines, etc., to change the appearance each month.

ON-GOING
BULLETIN BOARDS
(continued)

3. Select a board to be a "Super Student" display. Enlarge a giant character to fill one side of the board. Label the top of the board "Super Students." Pin up student awards, 100% spelling tests, creative writing papers and fantastic math pages. To change the board each month, just change the character. No need to change the entire character just add an item or two. For September, put an apple in his hand. For October, add a jack o'lantern, trick or treat bag and a halloween mask. For November, how about a pilgrim's hat? December, you guessed it! A white beard and red knit cap.

Your students will be eager to discover what new costume you have created each month!

4. Birthday bulletin boards, classroom helpers, school announcement displays and reading group illustrations can all be created once before school starts and changed monthly with very little effort. With all these on-going ideas, you'll discover that all that bulletin board space seems smaller than you thought.

LETTERING AND
HEADINGS

Not every school has a letter machine that produces perfect 2" or 4" letters from construction paper. (There is such a thing, you know.) The rest of us will just have to use the old stencil and scissor method. But wait, there is an easier way!

1. Don't cut individual letters. They are difficult to pin up straight, anyway. Instead, hand print bulletin board titles and headings onto strips of colored paper. When it is time for the board to come down, simply roll it up to use again next year.

Use your imagination. Try cloud shapes and cartoon bubbles. They will all look great.

LETTERING AND
HEADINGS
(continued)

2. Hand lettering is not that difficult, even if your printing is not up to penmanship standards. Print block letters with a felt marker. Draw big dots at the ends of each letter. This will hide any mistakes and add a charming touch to the overall effect.

If you are still afraid about free handing it, try this nifty idea: Cut a strip of poster board about 28" X 6". Down the center of the strip cut a window with an art knife measuring 20" X 2". There you have it, a perfect stencil for any lettering job. All you do is write your letters with a felt marker within the window slot. Don't worry about uniformity, just fill up the entire window heighth with your letters. Move your poster board strip along as you go. The letters will always remain straight and even because the poster board window is straight.

3. If you must cut individual letters, use this idea:

Cut numerous sheets of construction paper into 4½" X 6" squares. (Laminate first if you can.) Cut letters as shown in the illustration. No need to measure, irregular letters will look creative not messy.

Notes

Calendar

- SEPTEMBER CALENDAR AND ACTIVITIES
- CALENDAR TOPPERS
- BLANK CALENDAR

September

September

FLOWER: Morning Glory
BIRTHSTONE: Sapphire

1   NATIONAL FREEDOM DAY commemorates the day in 1865 when
     President Lincoln proposed an amendment to end slavery.
     (Read your students the 13th Amendment of the Constitu-
     tion of the United States.)

2   The U.S. TREASURY DEPARTMENT was established by Congress
     in 1789. (Review with your students those famous persons
     represented on our currency.)

3   LOUIS SULLIVAN is credited with inventing the first SKY-
     SCRAPER. He was born on this day in 1856. (Ask your
     students to research the world's tallest skyscraper.)

4   HAPPY BIRTHDAY! LOS ANGELES, CALIFORNIA! On this day
     in 1781, forty-four Mexican people colonized what was
     then a tiny settlement. (Ask students to find the mean-
     ing of the Spanish words "Los Angeles.")

5   The FIRST CONTINENTAL CONGRESS met on this day in 1774.
     (Students may wish to find the city in which the Congress
     met on the classroom map.)

6   JANE ADDAMS, American social worker, was born on this day
     in 1860. (Ask students to find out more about her.)

7   The famous American artist, GRANDMA MOSES, was born on
     this day in 1860. (Find a print of one of her paintings
     and share it with the class.)

8   Today is the CHEROKEE NATIONAL HOLIDAY. It commemorates
     the arrival of the Cherokee Nation at the Indian Terri-
     tory of Oklahoma. (Ask students to find the state of
     Oklahoma and capital city on the classroom map.)

9   ABRAHAM LINCOLN received a license to practice law in
     the state of Illinois on this day in 1836. (Ask students
     what they know of Lincoln's education.)

10   JOSE FELICIANO was born on this day in 1945. This gifted
     musician has overcome his blindness to become a successful
     master of music. (Ask students to find out about other
     disabled persons who have overcome their handicaps.)

September

11   HENRY HUDSON, a Dutch explorer, discovered Manhattan Island in 1609. (Ask students to find out what was named after him.)

12   JESSE OWENS, acclaimed American Olympic athlete, was born on this day in 1913. (Ask students to find out in what event he competed.)

13   MARGARET CHASE SMITH was elected to the Senate on this day in 1948. (Ask students why her election to the Senate was so important.)

14   On this day in 1814, FRANCES SCOTT KEY wrote the words of The Star Spangled Banner. (Review the words of the first verse of our national anthem with your students.)

15   Today, Japan celebrates OLD PEOPLE'S DAY, to honor the elderly. (Ask students to suggest ways in which we can honor our elderly.)

16   MEXICO began her battle for independence from Spain on this day in 1810. El Dia De Independencia! (Teach your students to count from 1-5 in Spanish.)

17   Today is CITIZENSHIP DAY in honor of the anniversary of the signing of the U.S. Constitution. (As a class, write your own classroom constitution.)

18   GEORGE WASHINGTON laid the cornerstone of the U.S. CAPITOL in Washington, D.C. on this day in 1793. (Students often confuse the White House with the Capitol Building. Show them pictures of each and explain the difference.)

19   MICKEY MOUSE appeared for the first time in 1928 in the movie Steamboat Willie. (Ask students if they know who created the character of Mickey Mouse.)

20   The famous explorer FERDINAND MAGELLAN set sail on this day in 1519. (Ask students to research his voyage and point it out on the classroom map.)

21   On this day, the people of ARGENTINA celebrate the coming of SPRING! (Ask students to find out how this could be true.)

22   Today is PEN PAL DAY all over the world. (Have your students exchange letters with the class next door.)

23   AUTUMN officially begins in the Northern Hemisphere. (Ask students to name at least three trees that lose their leaves in the autumn.)

24   Today marks the anniversary of the first observance of AMERICAN INDIAN DAY, in 1912. (Ask students to use reference books and find six names of American Indian tribes.)

25   The Spanish explorer BALBOA discovered the Pacific Ocean on this day in 1513. (Balboa made his discovery in an unusual way. Ask students to find out how he did it.)

26   JOHNNY APPLESEED was born on this day in 1776. (Ask students to find out his real name.)

27   A woman was arrested for smoking a cigarette on this day in 1904 in New York city. (Ask students to write a paragraph about their feelings about smoking, or women's rights.)

28   Today is a national holiday in TAIWAN. It's the birthday of the great Chinese teacher, CONFUCIUS. (Find one of his proverbs and share it with the class.)

29   ENRICO FERMI was born on this day in 1901. He was an Italian physicist who pioneered work on the atomic bomb. (Ask students how they feel about atomic weapons.)

30   BABE RUTH hit his 60th home run of the year on this day in 1927. (How many of your students know for which team Babe Ruth played?)

DON'T FORGET THESE OTHER IMPORTANT HOLIDAYS:

LABOR DAY   (Celebrated on the first Monday in September.)

ROSH HASHANAH   (The Jewish New Year is celebrated on the first and second day of the Jewish month of Tishri.)

GRANDPARENT'S DAY   (Celebrated the first Sunday of September.)

SEPTEMBER

September

sun	mon	tue	wed	thu	fri	sat

Let's Get Ready!

- BE PREPARED
- THE FIRST DAY
- STUDENT QUESTIONNAIRE
- CLASSROOM CODE
- READER OF THE WEEK
- BACK TO SCHOOL BINGO
- WORD FIND
- WELCOME OWL
- TRANSPORTATION TAGS
- WELCOME VISOR
- WELCOME DOOR SIGN

Be Prepared

THINGS TO DO <u>BEFORE</u> THE FIRST DAY OF SCHOOL

ROOM ENVIRONMENT

___ Prepare or purchase bulletin board materials

___ Make decisions of where to post materials

___ Make classroom "Welcome" sign

___ Set up learning centers, display tables and student work areas.

___ _____

___ _____

SUPPLIES

___ Purchase or obtain class supplies from the school office

__ Writing paper
__ Drawing paper
__ Construction paper
__ Duplicating masters
__ Duplicating paper
__ Pencils/pens
__ Crayons
__ Paste/glue
__ Stapler and staples
__ Paper clips
__ Rubber bands
__ Straight pins
__ Transparent tape
__ Manilla folders
__ Marking pens
__ Rulers
__ Art supplies
__ Grade book
__ Lesson plan book
__ Seating chart
__ Attendance materials
__ Textbooks/workbooks

__ _____
__ _____
__ _____

STUDENT PREPARATIONS

___ Make student name tags

___ Prepare materials for student take-home the first day

__ Emergency cards
__ School rules
__ Classroom rules
__ Bus regulations
__ Letter to parents
__ Classroom schedule

___ Prepare class list

___ Prepare seating chart

___ Check records for students with special needs

___ Select reading groups

GETTING ORGANIZED

___ Post class discipline rules

___ Arrange student desks

___ Pin up bulletin boards

___ Write lesson plans for the first week

___ Duplicate material needed for the first week

___ Write daily schedule and your name on the board

___ Prepare files for.....

__ Correspondence - parents
__ School bulletins
__ Substitute teacher

__ _____
__ _____
__ _____

The First Day

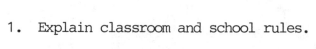

1. Explain classroom and school rules.

2. Explain your system for classroom helpers.

3. Explain your grading policy.

4. Explain homework policies and your expectations.

5. Discuss the use of learning centers, classroom supplies and equipment.

6. Explain the procedures you wish used in collecting and passing out papers and supplies.

7. Check children's lunch arrangements before lunch time.

8. Check children's transportation arrangements.

9. Explain cafeteria procedures and rules.

10. Distribute books and materials and discuss their care.

11. Issue pencils, crayons, rulers, etc.

12. As a class, tour the school grounds and meet school personnel.

13. Participate with the class in a "Getting To Know YOU" activity.

14. Involve students in a creative writing assignment or a student questionnaire. (This is one way to assess students' ability quickly.) Save this assignment to evaluate hand writing improvement during the school year.

15. Hold a class discussion on their expectation of the new school year.

16. Discuss the first day of school by praising good behavior and offering suggestion for improvements.

17. Discuss planned field trips, classroom rewards and class parties.

18. Pass out parent materials that need to be taken home. Discuss which forms need to be signed and returned to school.

Student Questionnaire

1. What do you like most about school? _____
   _____

2. What do you like to do in your spare time? _____
   _____

3. What are some things you know a lot about? _____
   _____

4. What kinds of books do you like most? _____
   _____

5. What are some things about which you would like to know more? _____
   _____

6. What interesting places have you visited? _____
   _____

7. What are some places you would like to visit? _____
   _____

8. If you could be a famous person, who would you be? _____
   _____

9. Do you like music? What kind? _____
   _____

10. What are you good at in school? _____
    _____

11. What do you think you might need extra help with in school? _____
    _____

12. What is your favorite.....
    Food? _____   Sport? _____
    Color? _____   Place? _____
    TV Show? _____   Movie? _____

13. Who is your favorite.....
    Celebrity? _____   Friend? _____

14. Complete these sentences.
    I am happiest when _____
    _____
    I am saddest when _____
    _____

Classroom Code

One way to achieve a successful classroom management program is to utilize a "Classroom Code of Conduct." Discuss with your class the elements of good class behavior and write their responses on the chalkboard. After the class has reached agreement on the classroom code, recopy it onto a sheet of poster board and display it in a conspicuous place. Suggestions are as follows:

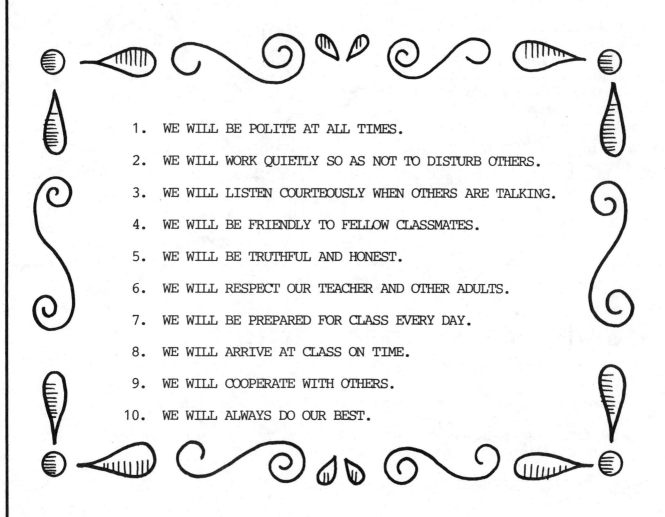

1. WE WILL BE POLITE AT ALL TIMES.

2. WE WILL WORK QUIETLY SO AS NOT TO DISTURB OTHERS.

3. WE WILL LISTEN COURTEOUSLY WHEN OTHERS ARE TALKING.

4. WE WILL BE FRIENDLY TO FELLOW CLASSMATES.

5. WE WILL BE TRUTHFUL AND HONEST.

6. WE WILL RESPECT OUR TEACHER AND OTHER ADULTS.

7. WE WILL BE PREPARED FOR CLASS EVERY DAY.

8. WE WILL ARRIVE AT CLASS ON TIME.

9. WE WILL COOPERATE WITH OTHERS.

10. WE WILL ALWAYS DO OUR BEST.

After you have displayed the chart in the classroom, have each student sign his or her name at the bottom with a bright colored felt marker.

(Note: Always try to list elements in a positive manner and not the disturbing "Don't do...." method.)

Reader of the Week

Encourage confidence in oral reading by beginning a "Reader of the Week" activity. Ask each student to select a short story, article or passage from a longer book to be read aloud in class. Each student should prepare before hand by reading the piece at home to his/her parents. When the student feels ready, he or she may sign up to read that week. The other students must also be prepared to listen quietly and appreciatively. Emphasize, also, how the reader should be conscious of his voice, volume, expression and rate.

Each "Reader of the Week" should be awarded a certificate of completion with his/her name and book title. A special "Reader of the Week" bulletin board can be used to display the certificates.

By beginning this activity in September, you will experience a year's worth of oral reading enjoyment.

Back to School Bingo

This game offers an exciting way to welcome students back to school. Give each child a copy of the bingo words listed below or write the words on the chalkboard. Ask students to write any 24 words on his or her bingo card. Use the same directions you might use for regular bingo.

BACK TO SCHOOL BINGO WORDS

SCHOOL	FLAG	PRINCIPAL	TEACHER
CLASSROOM	CUSTODIAN	PENCIL	INSTRUCTION
CRAYONS	FIRE DRILL	RULER	LEARN
SEPTEMBER	SOCIAL STUDIES	LANGUAGE	GRADES
GLUE	PLAYGROUND	SCISSORS	MENU
CAFETERIA	KINDERGARTEN	MATHEMATICS	PAINT
NOTEBOOK	CHALKBOARD	ERASER	CLAY
MUSIC	REPORT CARD	SPELLING	BOOKS
BUS	STUDENTS	PENMANSHIP	LESSON
ART	RECESS	READING	SCIENCE

BACK TO SCHOOL BINGO

FREE

Back to School Word Find

```
A S D F R T H K L P I O S C H O O L D T
W E F G T Y H J E D U C A T I O N W E H
Q W E F L F D F G T Y H U J I K O U O
P R T B A S C L A S S T H N M V X Z S M
R T E R C V T Y U S P E L L I N G L I E
I W Q D H R P L A Y G R O U N D Y B R W
N S C I E N C E G H J K V M C D R T Y O
C Y H F R T N L P S T U D E N T S F G R
I Y H J T M H U K A R T T H J U T F R K
P D R G H A D F D R T Y U J N M U H U L
A W R I T I N G J U M A T H G Y D H U J
L T H U J K I S C F T V G S E R Y G M R
R E A D I N G G H N V X Z A M U S I C W
K D M S D V B G T R E W Q X C V B N M J
```

ACTIVITY 1

FIND THE FOLLOWING "BACK TO SCHOOL" WORDS: SCHOOL, EDUCATION, HOMEWORK, TEACHER, PRINCIPAL, CLASS, STUDY, PLAYGROUND, MUSIC, STUDENTS, READING, SPELLING, MATH, ART, SCIENCE, WRITING.

WRITE A SHORT PARAGRAPH USING AT LEAST EIGHT OF THE WORDS LISTED ABOVE.

_____

_____

_____

_____

_____

_____

Welcome Owl

Children may write their own thoughts about school on the owl's wings.

stick

Make the "Welcome Owl" from brown construction paper. Fold along dotted lines. Attach an ice cream stick as a handle.

Welcome to School!

Transportation Tags

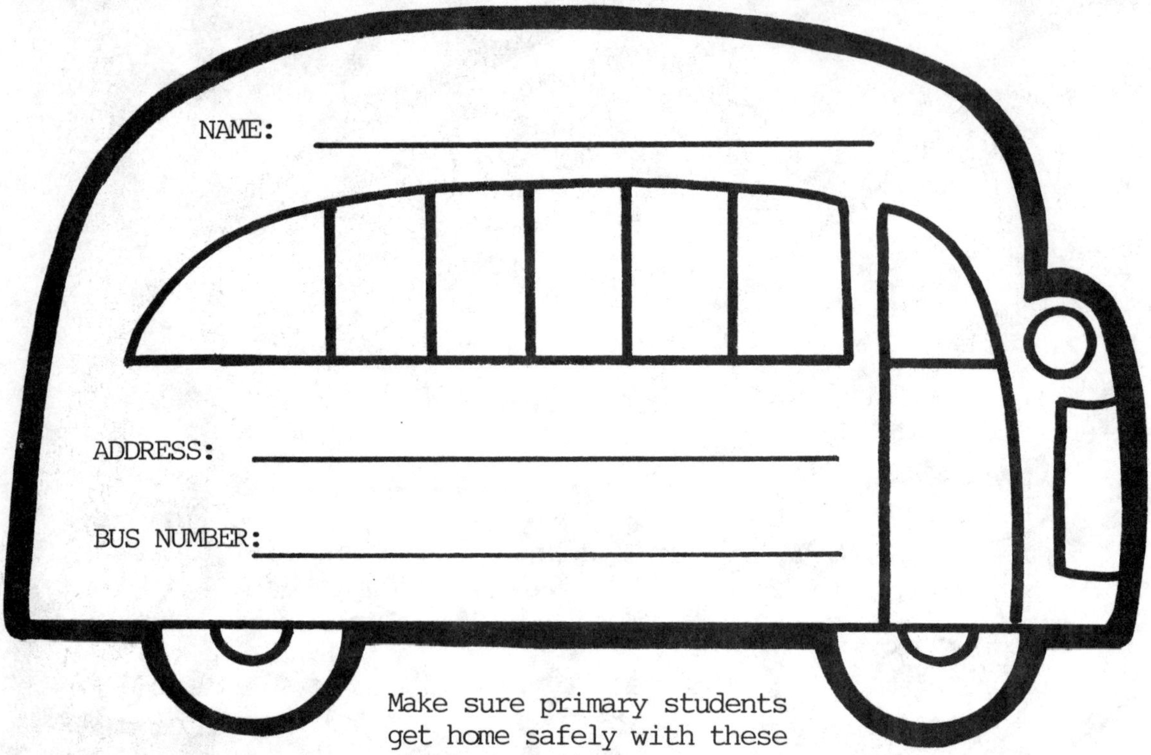

NAME: _____

ADDRESS: _____

BUS NUMBER: _____

Make sure primary students get home safely with these simple name tags.

Bus drivers will love you for it!

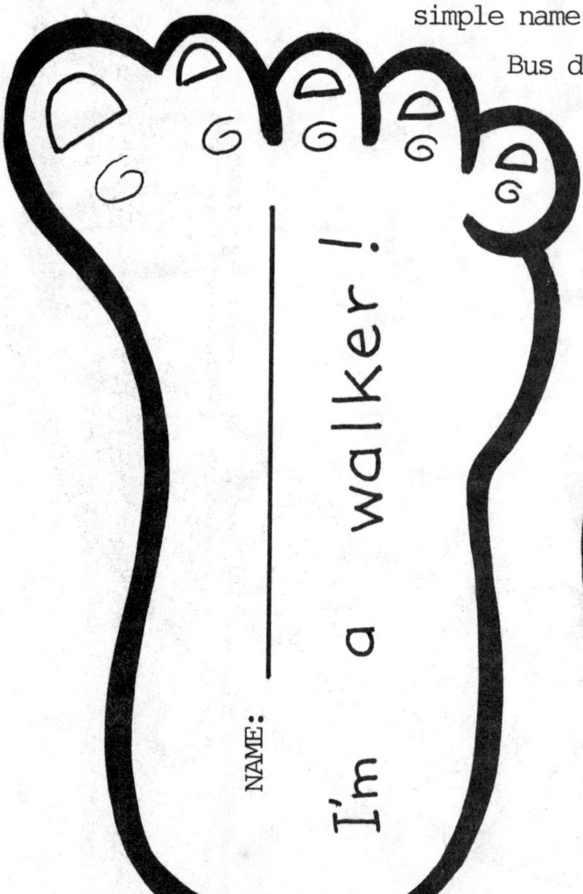

NAME: _____

I'm a walker!

NAME: _____

Some one picks me up!

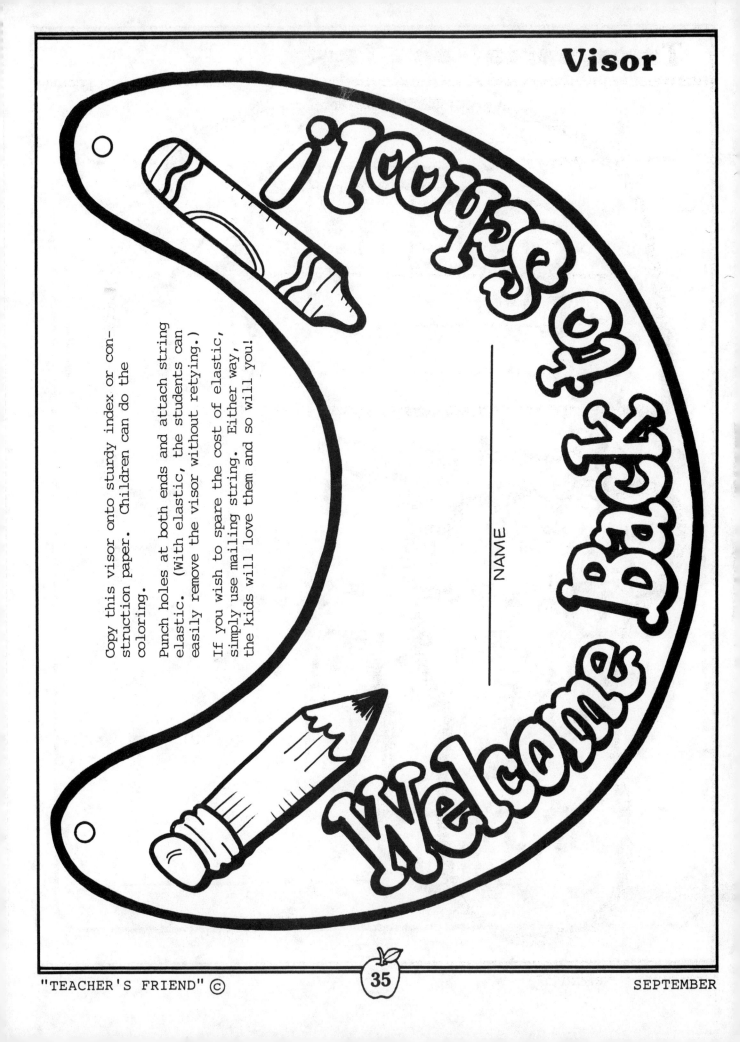

¡Back to School!

Welcome Back

NAME

Copy this visor onto sturdy index or construction paper. Children can do the
coloring.

Punch holes at both ends and attach string
elastic. (With elastic, the students can
easily remove the visor without retying.)

If you wish to spare the cost of elastic,
simply use mailing string. Either way,
the kids will love them and so will you!

Door Sign

Mount this "Welcome Back" sign on poster board and color.

Cut out the circle and hang on your classroom door knob.

Hi WELCOME to room

That's My Name!

- NAME HEADBANDS
- NAME DISCUSSIONS
- CLOTHESPIN NAME TAGS
- CROSSWORD NAMES
- NAME BRANDS
- NAME CRITTERS
- NAME LIMERICKS AND POEMS
- NEWS NAMES
- NAME CARDS
- NAME GAME
- NAME TAG DISPLAYS
- NAME TAGS
- NAME TRAIN

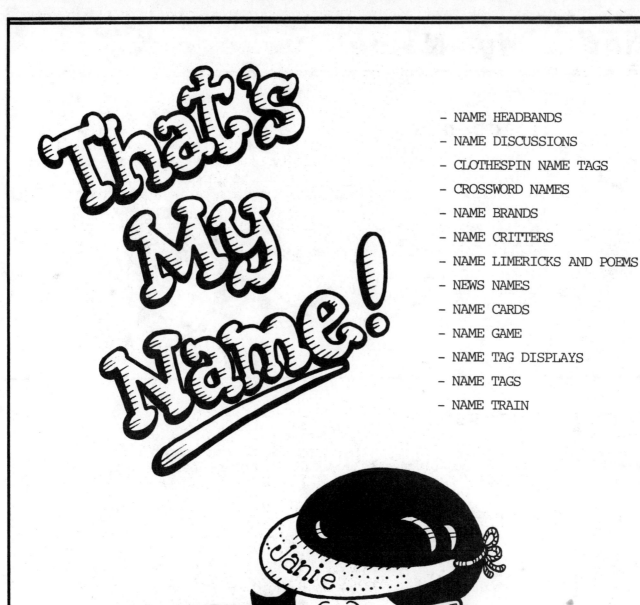

That's My Name!

Name Headbands

Name tags are particularly helpful the first day of school, but by the end of the day they have either become lost or damaged beyond repair. For a practical solution, try name headbands. They are easily made from strips of tag board or laminated construction paper. Measure the strips to fit each child and staple in place. Write the child's name on the front of the headband with colored marker. The children will adore wearing them and you'll love the way they last all week long!

Name Discussions

Discuss with your students the origin and meaning of some common first and last names. Encourage discussion by asking how they feel about their names.

"Do you like your name?"

"How do you feel when you see your name in print?"

"Does anyone ever mispronounce your name?"

"If you could choose any name, what would it be? Why?"

"Have you ever discovered what your name means?"

"Were you named after someone? Who?"

"Do you have a nickname? How did you get it?"

Clothespin Name Tags

On the first day of school, let your students find unique "name tags" at their desks. WOODEN CLOTHESPINS!

Wooden clothespins, with student names written with colored marker, can be a great way to assign temporary seating arrangements. Each child will also be thrilled to find this small personalized gift at his/her desk.

These special "name tags" can also be used to identify items brought to school, art projects, and of course papers to be sent home to parents.

That's My Name!

Crossword Names

Instruct students to create crossword puzzles with their own names. Begin by having them write their first names down the center of a piece of lined writing paper. Pupils then add hobbies, favorite colors, personal traits, etc., to each letter of their name.

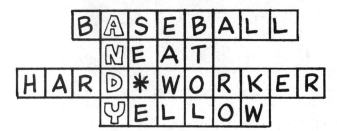

Questions or clues pertaining to the crosswords may be added at the bottom of the page. Have students exchange puzzles to be solved. (Older students might like to use their first and last names in the crossword.)

Name Brands

Many manufactured products are commonly known by the people who invented them. For example, bluejeans are often referred to as "Levi's," a piano as a "Steinway," and an automobile as a "Ford." Instruct your students to invent a product that would carry their name. Begin by having them draw a picture of the product and then write a paragraph explaining their reason why this product was their choice.

Name Critters

Ask the students to write their names in crayon, using large letters, on pieces of art paper. The children may then create their own name critter using the outline of the letters.

Students might also like to scramble the letters in their name first before drawing the critter. Children can then trade papers and try to guess the critter's name.

That's My Name!

Name Limericks

After introducing the concepts of limerick writing, ask students to create their own limericks using their own names. Older students will love this activity.

For example a student might write:

> There once was a lady named Ann,
>
> Who constantly used a large fan.
>
> When the weather was hot
>
> She used it a lot
>
> Even though she kept getting a tan.

Name Poems

Using letters in their names, students can describe themselves with this simple writing assignment. Ask each child to write their name vertically on the left-hand side of a sheet of paper. Instruct students to write poems about themselves using the letters of their names. Each letter begins the first word of each line.

For example:

R obbie is a happy boy.

O nly now and then is he sad.

B est ball player in class.

B eautiful blue eyes.

I nteresting and smart.

E xtra special person!

News Names

Instruct students to search newspapers and magazines for current articles about people who share their names. Ask students to make a list of the people they find and the reasons for them being in the news.

Assign a short paper on why they are happy or unhappy to have a first or last name in common with such people.

That's My Name!

Name Cards

Write each child's first name in bold letters on a large index card. Ask students to do the following activities:

- Alphabetize the cards.

- Find names with the same first letter.

- Find the shortest name.

- Find the longest name.

- Find names that rhyme.

- Find names with the same vowel sounds.

The same might be done with student last names. Store the cards in a file box. Students may perform the tasks at their desks after classroom work is completed.

Name Game

Good listening skills are required to play this "Get Acquainted" game.

"Hi! I'm Cindy. I love to go roller skating!"

Prepare a name tag for each child in class and place them in a bag or bowl. Instruct students to sit in a circle on the floor. A volunteer must also be chosen to draw a name tag. The student whose name is drawn stands up, tells his name and shares what he loves to do best. When every name tag has been drawn and each student has had a chance to speak, return the tags to the bag. This time as the tags are drawn, students must give the name of the classmate on their right and what he or she likes best to do.

A variation of this activity could be simply to eliminate the name tags and call on each student in turn. Each child must repeat what every child before him has said before telling about himself.

Name Tag Displays

Name tags can do more then simply identify students. They can serve to motivate children by adding to the creative atmosphere of the classroom.

Try some of these ideas:

Plant a tree limb in a pail of plaster of paris. Decorative name tags can be hung from the branches each month. You might use apple name tags in September, Jack O'Lanterns in October, and so on. Children can be given the name tags at the end of the month as an award or they may be asked to attach an original poem to the back.

A box of small white envelopes is all you need for these name tags.

"Address" each envelope with the name of each student. Use stickers or trading stamps as postage. Arrange them around a cut paper mail box which includes your name and room number.

Provide each child with a white paper plate and ask them to draw and color a self portrait. Instruct them to fill the entire plate with the drawing of their face.

Pin the finished plates to a class bulletin board. The word "WELCOME" should already be in place at the top of the board. Pin large paper-cut bow name tags to each paper plate. Bowties for boys and hair-bows for girls.

Name Tags

Use this crayon and pencil pattern for back to school name tags.

These useful patterns can also be enlarged for bulletin board displays.

Name Train

Use this pattern to display a "Name Train" along the top of the classroom chalkboard. Each boxcar contains a different student's name. Add stickers or stars for outstanding accomplishments.

My "Me" Book!

MY "ME" BOOK is a complete individual booklet designed for the primary student.

Make enough copies for every child in class. Pages may be printed two-sided. Staple the pages together in booklet form.

Children will love discovering themselves with their own "Me" book.

My "Me" Book

This is my name: _____

The End

I finished writing My "Me" Book

Month _____

Day _____

Year _____

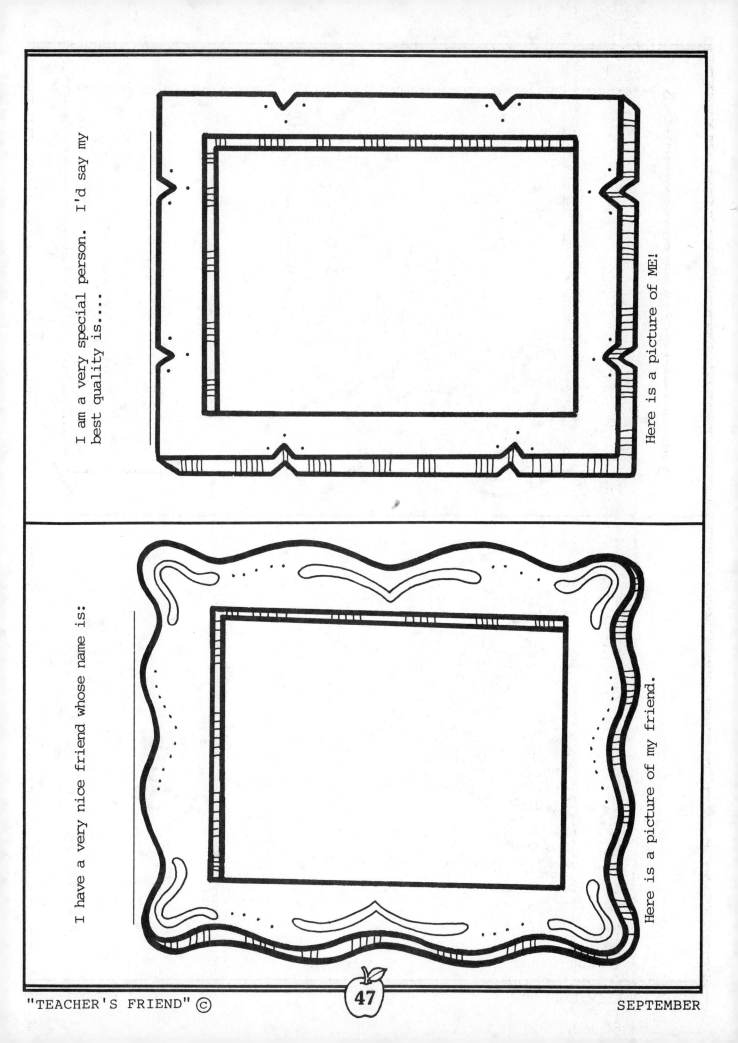

I am a very special person. I'd say my best quality is.....

Here is a picture of ME!

I have a very nice friend whose name is:

Here is a picture of my friend.

I picked a friend to help measure
my body.

My friend is _____

My foot is _____ inches.

My arm is _____ inches.

My finger is _____ inches.

My nose is _____ inches.

My wrist is _____ inches.

My leg is _____ inches.

My body is _____ inches.

There is one thing you should
know.

Am I a boy?
Or a girl?
I'll tell you......

I am a _____

This is my address.

_____
number   street

_____
city   state

My phone number is:

_____

This is a picture of my family.

Their names are:

_____ _____

_____ _____

_____ _____

I have _____ sisters.

I have _____ brothers.

I live in a:

☐ HOUSE

☐ APARTMENT

☐ MOBILE HOME

☐ DUPLEX

☐ TREE HOUSE

It looks like this:

I counted my teeth.

I have _____ on the top.

I have _____ on the bottom.

I have lost this many baby teeth.

My hair looks like this:

The color of my hair is _____.

My birthday is:

Month _____

Day _____

Year _____

Happy Birthday

Here are the number of candles I will have on my cake next birthday.

This is the color of my eyes.

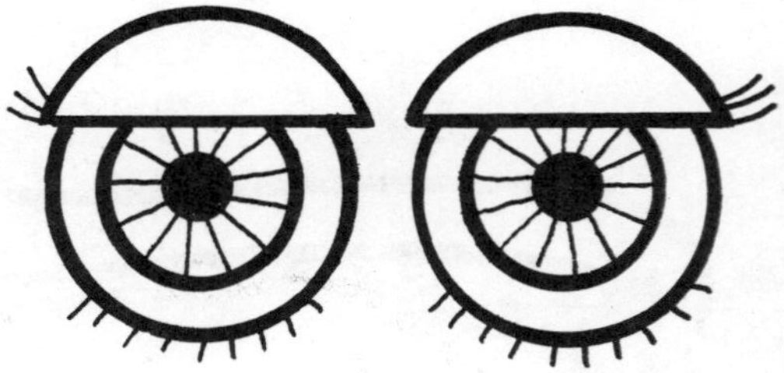

☐ I do have freckles

☐ I don't have freckles

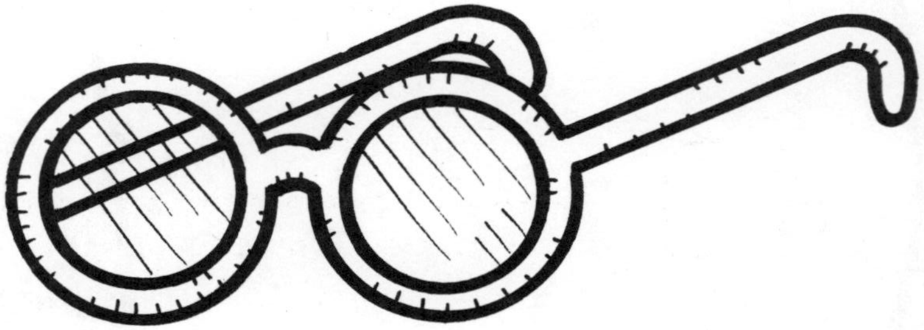

☐ I do wear glasses

☐ I don't wear glasses

My favorite meal is:

Mmmm

☐ BREAKFAST

☐ LUNCH

☐ DINNER

Here is a picture of my favorite food!

But, please don't give me any

Yuk!

_____

When I grow up I'd like to be a: _____

Here is a drawing of me when I've grown up.

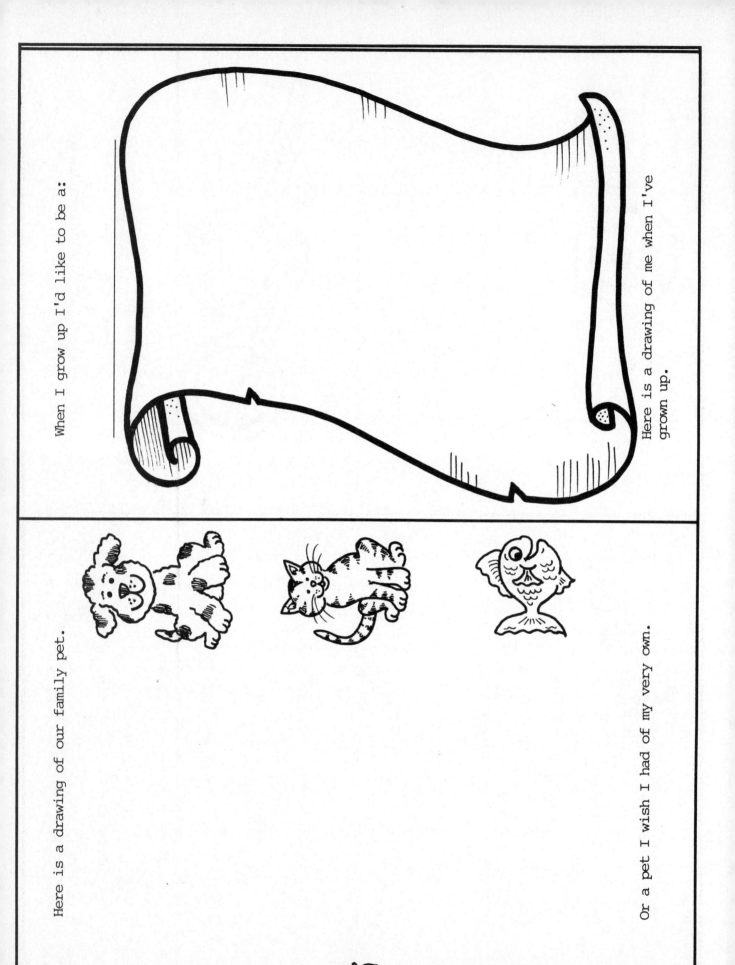

Here is a drawing of our family pet.

Or a pet I wish I had of my very own.

There are a lot of things I like.

These are my favorites.

NUMBER

TOY

GAME

HOLIDAY

COLOR

DAY OF THE WEEK

SEASON

FOOD

BOOK

T.V. SHOW

This is my hand.

I write with my _____ hand.

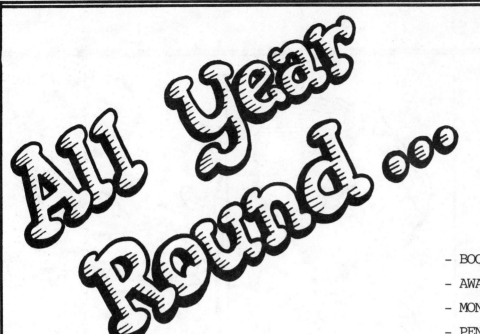

All Year Round ...

- BOOKMARKS
- AWARDS AND CERTIFICATES
- MONTHLY SYMBOLS
- PENCIL TOPPERS
- TESTING SIGN
- OWL PUPPET
- CLASSROOM CHARACTERS
- VISORS

Fish FOR Facts WITH Books

_____
Name

_____
Room

Read a Book! Pass the Word...

_____
Name

Find out what's cooking at the Library

_____
Name

_____
Room

_____
Name

WAS A REALLY
"WISE" OWL
TODAY!

_____
date

_____
Name

WAS A REAL BOOKWORM TODAY!

_____   _____
date   teacher

_____
Name

REALLY DID A GREAT JOB
TODAY!

_____
date

_____
Name

WAS A PERFECT STUDENT TODAY!

SEPTEMBER

Certificate of Achievement

is presented to

For Superior Achievement and Excellence

TEACHER

PRINCIPAL

SEPTEMBER

Certificate of Award

This award of distinction is presented to

_____

in recognition of

_____

Date _____

Monthly Symbols

These monthly symbols can be used in a variety of ways.

NAME TAGS: Reproduce enough copies on colored paper for every student in class.

CALENDAR DATES: Make one copy for every day of the month. Add numbers and create a bulletin board calendar.

NOTES TO PARENTS: Write messages home when a student has done well in class.

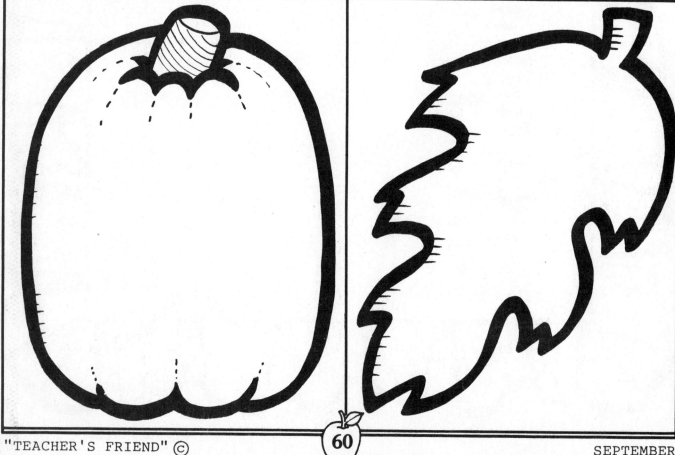

Monthly Symbols

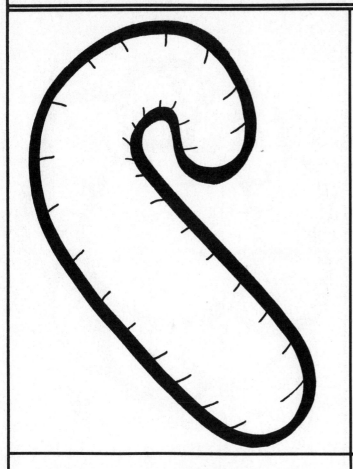

Monthly Symbols

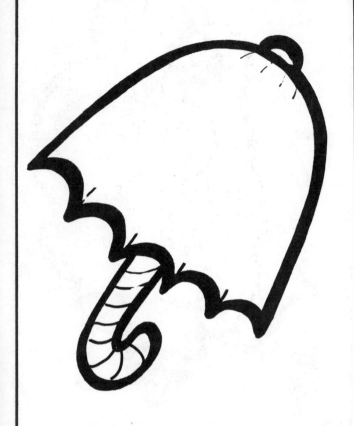

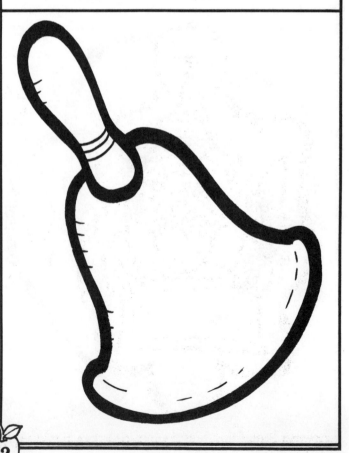

Pencil Toppers

Reproduce these "Pencil Toppers" onto construction or index paper. Color and cut out. Use an art knife to cut through the Xs.

Slide a pencil through both Xs, as shown.

Use as classroom awards, back to school gifts or birthday treats.

Door Sign

Mount this "Testing" sign on poster board and color.

Cut out the circle and hang on your classroom door knob.

Please don't disturb. We're Testing!

Owl Puppet

Cut this owl puppet pattern from construction paper.

Glue the two pieces to a small brown paper lunch bag.

A "Back to School" greeting can be written on the front of each owl.

Classroom Characters

Enlarged, these cute characters can be used in bulletin board displays. You might wish to use them to announce reading groups or label learning centers.

As they are, they can be used as booklet covers or mini display characters.

You might even like to make one of them poster board size and attach it to your classroom door. A word of "welcome", your name and room number would be all you would need.

However you choose to use them, you'll find them to be a real asset to any room environment.

SEPTEMBER

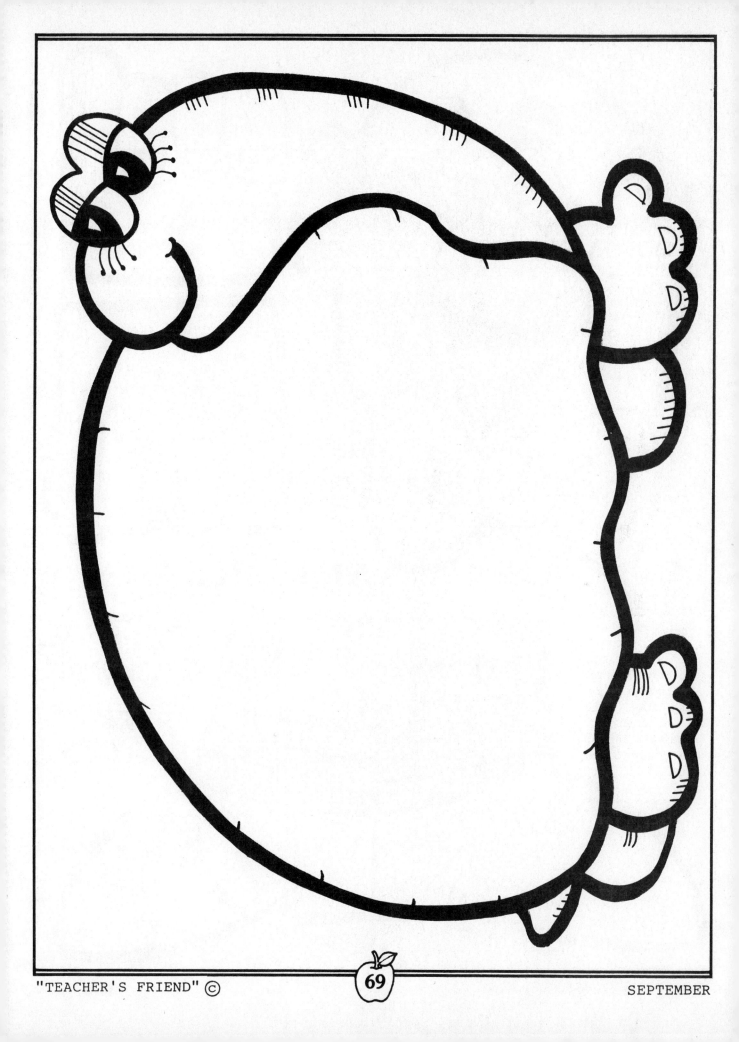

SEPTEMBER

Cut
along
dotted
lines.

Sign Man

Enlarge this "Sign Man" pattern onto posterboard. Cut out and color. Display him as illustrated on the class bulletin board. Change his "sign" as needed each month.

Welcome

Copy these visors onto sturdy index or construction paper. Children can do the coloring.

Punch holes at both ends and attach string elastic. (With elastic, the students can easily remove the visors without retying.)

If you wish to spare the cost of elastic, simply use mailing string. Either way, the kids will love them and so will you!

HAPPY BIRTHDAY

STUDENT OF THE WEEK

Apple Time

Johnny Appleseed Day
September 26th

Apple Seeds

Johnny Appleseed

"Johnny Appleseed" was born on September 26, 1776, in the state of Massachusetts. His real name was John Chapman, but he was given the nickname "Johnny Appleseed" because he dedicated his life to the planting and pruning of apple trees. He traveled hundreds of miles in what are now the states of Ohio, Indiana and Illinois. Wherever he went he planted apple seeds that he carried in a sack on his back. He became good friends with the Indians and the early settlers across the frontier. "Johnny Appleseed" is a celebrated hero in the legends of the American westward movement.

To honor "Johnny Appleseed" and have some fun at the same time, make applesauce in your classroom. Here is a simple recipe.

APPLESAUCE

For each quart of peeled and
sliced apples, use the following:

1 cup water
½ cup sugar
1 tsp. lemon juice
¼ tsp. cinnamon
pinch of salt

Cook all ingredients until tender.
Mash the apples with a potato
masher or electric mixer, adding
more sugar if desired.
Serve cold.

ANSWER THESE TRUE AND FALSE QUESTIONS ABOUT JOHNNY APPLESEED.

T   F   Johnny Appleseed was born in the state of Ohio.

T   F   Johnny Appleseed's real name was John Chapman.

T   F   Johnny Appleseed was given his nickname because he loved to
             eat apples.

T   F   Johnny Appleseed did not like the Indians.

T   F   Johnny Appleseed was a real man.

ACTIVITY 2

Apple Mobile

Use this pattern to make apple core mobiles to hang in the classroom. Cut two tops, two centers, two bottoms and two stems and leaves from construction paper. Use red or yellow paper for the apple, white for the core and green for the leaf.

Glue a piece of yarn down the middle of the apple and hang.

After sampling pieces of fresh apples, children may wish to save the apple seeds and glue them in place on the core.

To play this game make twelve red apples and one green apple from construction paper.

Add multiplication tables, vocabulary words or review questions to the back of the paper apples. Place all the apples in a small wicker basket.

Two students lay all thirteen apples on a table, question side down. Each player takes turns taking an apple avoiding the "green apple."

Each player must answer correctly before keeping the apple. A self-correcting answer sheet should be included.

THE BIG APPLE

Cut pairs of large apples from red and white construction paper. On the white apple, write an activity that the children can do pertaining to apples. Cover each white apple with its matching red apple. Staple them together at the top and display on a bulletin board.

Children can come to the board during free time. After lifting a chosen red apple, the child returns to his/her desk to do the activity.

Apple Puppet

Apple Booklet

NAME

Copy this pattern onto a folded sheet of construction paper. Place lined writing paper inside. Cut all layers of paper at one time. Staple at the fold.

Students may write their own "Apple" stories inside.

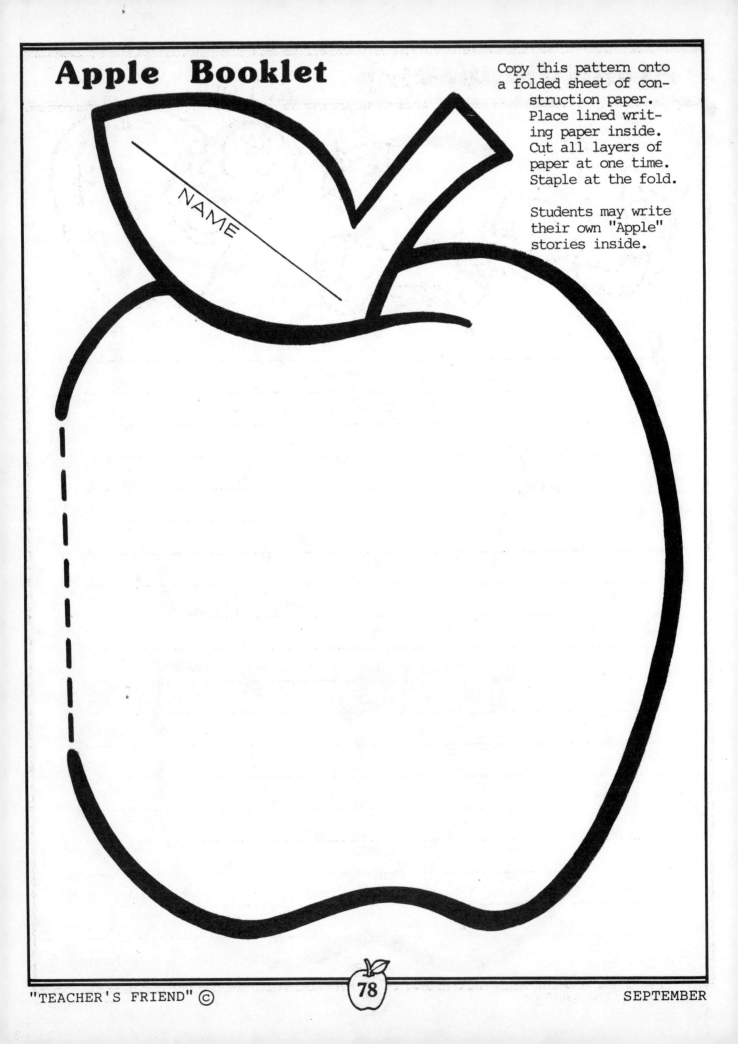

Creative Writing

_____

_____

_____

_____

_____

_____

_____

_____

_____

_____

_____

_____

_____

_____

_____

_____

_____

_____

_____

_____

Color Page

Teachers:

Add your
own math
problems
to the apples in
the tree. Children
can color the pic-
ture after work is
completed.

Mexican Independence

September 16th

FIESTA TIME

Mexican Independence

In the United States of America, we celebrate the 4th of July as our Day of Independence. Mexico has two "Independence Days!" September 16 is a special holiday because it marks a vital decision by the Mexican people to be free from the European nations. May 5, Cinco de Mayo, signifies the day that the tiny Mexican army defeated the French at the battle of Puebla. Even though September 16 is considered Mexican Independence Day, both holidays are of great importance to the Mexican people.

After the explorers of Europe discovered North America, the Indians of Mexico were treated as slaves and their once rich cities and towns devastated. Enormous shipments of Mexico's gold and silver were taken across the Atlantic Ocean. The country of Spain claimed that Mexico belonged to them.

During the late 18th century, Spain attempted to establish their own rulers in Mexico. The Spaniards called their new colony "New Spain."

Finally, on September 16, 1810, an Indian priest named Miguel Hidalgo y Costilla spoke out against the Spanish government. He demanded that the Mexican Indians be given their rights and the freedom to govern themselves. Hidalgo's revolt was at first successful but lasted only a short time. He was arrested by the Spanish forces and executed. The leaders in Hidalgo's group tried to proclaim Mexico as a republic, separate from Spain. Their small group was soon defeated.

It was not until May 5, 1862 that the small Mexican army defeated the French army at the village of Puebla and began establishing the soon to be Mexican government.

Mexican Coat of Arms

The Aztecs of Mexico were the last of the great Indian tribes to arrive from the North. They settled in the Valley of Mexico more than one hundred years before Columbus found America.

It is said that Indian wisemen told the Aztec leaders to search for a certain sign. The sign was to be a live eagle perched on a cactus which grew from a large rock. The eagle would be holding a snake in its claw.

Finally in 1325, the sign they sought appeared. The eagle had been found on an island in a salty lake, and it was here that the Aztecs built the magnificent city, Tenochtitlan. Today it is called Mexico City.

The eagle in the coat of arms symbolizes strength and nobility; the snake, evilness and dishonor; the cactus, the Mexican soil.

The shield contains a branch of an evergreen oak and laurel. These are signs of honor and represent the heros of Mexico.

Map of Mexico

1. The United States of America is Mexico's neighbor to the north. Write UNITED STATES OF AMERICA on the proper line.

2. The Gulf of Mexico is east of Mexico. Write GULF OF MEXICO in the space to the east.

3. The Pacific Ocean is west of Mexico. Write PACIFIC OCEAN in the space to the west.

4. Mexico's neighbors to the south are Guatemala and Belize. Write the names GUATEMALA and BELIZE where they belong.

5. Our southern neighbor is Mexico. Write MEXICO in the central part of the map.

ACTIVITY 3

Spanish Word Find

FIND THESE SPANISH WORDS:

MEXICO
SERAPE
ESPANOL
MESA
ADIOS
SENOR
CASA
SENORITA
SOMBRERO
HACIENDA
BRONCO
FIESTA
TORTILLA
PIÑATA

```
R T E F I E S T A A C V B N M J K H G F D S A E
C S T Y U I D F G H J K L M N B M E X I C O P L
A W R T Y B G H D S R T H J K L O I U N B G T Y
S W C V A D I O S E T H Y U I K A S D F G H J T
A F V B N M C X Z R F S A W E P I N A T A M B V
A W E R T G H Y U A T G B F D S A E R T F D S A
W C X Z D F R T H P J U P L I W R T G H M R T Y
R T Y U D E R T H E K I B R O N C O E R E W T U
E S P A N O L E F G H L K D F M N B G F S W Y Y
K M S W C V B N M J K L P O I U Y T R E A E F R
W V F T H Y J U S Y U K I L O K T O R T I L L A
A S D F R T H Y O D R T H Y U J K I O L P L M K
W S A E C R F G M S A E T H A C I E N D A T H Y
E R Y H N G R F B K M Z X C V B N M L K J H G F
W E R T H Y J U R K S E T H Y J U I K L O Y H T
S E N O R S W E E A W E R T Y U I O P L K J H G
Q W E R T D C V R T G B N H Y U J M W R T Y H U
W S D E R T B V O A S E R C V S E N O R I T A Y
```

ACTIVITY 4

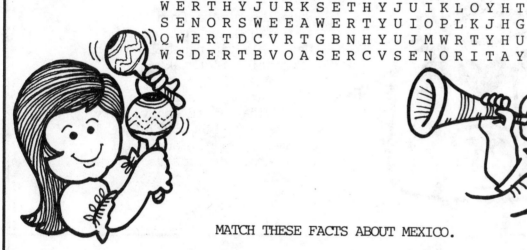

MATCH THESE FACTS ABOUT MEXICO.

MEXICO'S NEIGHBOR TO THE NORTH

MEXICAN INDEPENDENCE DAY

THE CAPITAL OF MEXICO

THE LANGUAGE OF THE MEXICAN PEOPLE

THEY BUILT THE MEXICAN PYRAMIDS

CINCO DE MAYO

THE COLORS OF THE MEXICAN FLAG

THE PRIEST WHO SPOKE AGAINST SPAIN

THE AZTECS

THE 5th OF MAY

RED, GREEN AND WHITE

UNITED STATES OF AMERICA

MEXICO CITY

SEPTEMBER 16th

FATHER HILDALGO

SPANISH

ACTIVITY 5

SEPTEMBER

Piñata & Bulletin Board

This Mexican Piñata will only take minutes to put together.

Place two or three large grocery bags inside one another and fill with treats. Fold the open ends of the bags around a sturdy coat hanger and tape or staple in place.

Cut shapes from construction paper and glue into place as illustrated. You could also let the students do the decorating. It is easy to turn the bag into a variety of creatures; parrot, pig, donkey and so on.

Hang the piñata from the ceiling with heavy cord or rope. Use a plastic baseball bat or broomstick to break.

It is not necessary to fill your piñata with candy. Try adding free homework night tickets, scratch and sniff stickers, new erasers and pencils.

"MAD ABOUT MEXICO"

Create a festive Mexican bulletin board with this simple idea.

Use patterns cut in shapes depicting Mexico. Have students trace the shapes on construction paper. Ask them to write creative stories or interesting facts about our neighbor to the south. Mount the title "Mad about Mexico" and display the new creations.

Creative Writing

MEXICAN INDEPENDENCE

_____

_____

_____

_____

_____

_____

_____

_____

_____

_____

_____

_____

_____

_____

_____

_____

_____

_____

_____

_____

_____

Color Page

Color this picture using the code below.

1 = VERDE

2 = ROJO

3 = MORADO

4 = AMARILLO

5 = NEGRO

6 = ANARANJADO

7 = AZUL

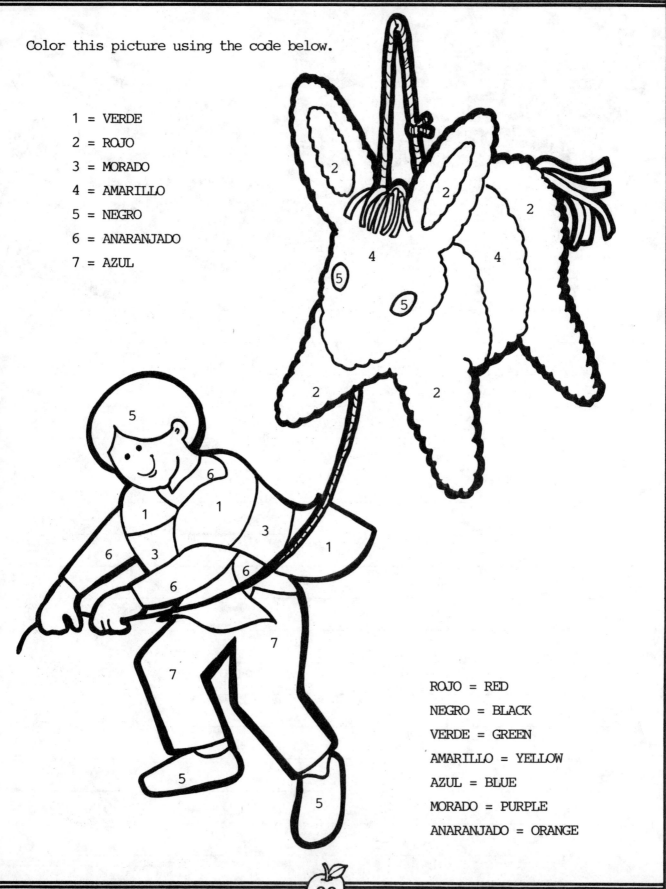

ROJO = RED

NEGRO = BLACK

VERDE = GREEN

AMARILLO = YELLOW

AZUL = BLUE

MORADO = PURPLE

ANARANJADO = ORANGE

American Indian Day

September 24th

Indian Cultural Areas

The name "Indians" was first given to the native Americans by Chistopher Columbus, who believed that the New World he discovered was part of the Indies, in Asia.

There are many, many tribes of American Indians. Each is very different from one another. Here is a listing of the seven main cultural areas in the United States.

THE SOUTHWEST - The Indians of this area lived in what is now the states of Arizona, New Mexico and Colorado. They were mostly farmers. They grew maize and beans. Most of them lived in towns made of terraced stone and adobe.

THE EASTERN WOODLANDS - This area covered the state of Minnesota and parts of southern Canada. It continued south to North Carolina and east to the Atlantic Ocean. This was a heavily forested area which provided the Indians with much game hunting and fishing. They also grew some crops.

THE SOUTHEAST - The Indians of this area lived in parts of Texas and throughout the south to the Atlantic shoreline in the east. These tribes raised some of their own deer for hunting. They also farmed and made beautiful handicrafts.

THE PLAINS - This is by far the largest Indian area. It extends from Canada to Mexico and the midwest to the Rocky Mountains. These Indians lived in small tribes which followed the herds of bison. They were great horsemen and are noted for their feathered headdresses and tepee houses.

THE PLATEAU REGION - The areas of Idaho and parts of Oregon and Washington was home to these Indians. They lived in sunken round houses in the winter and camped in mat homes in the summer. They fished the many rivers for salmon.

THE CALIFORNIA INTERMOUNTAIN - These Indians settled the valleys of Utah, Nevada and California. They lived in villages with thatched roofs and hunted sheep and deer. They were excellent basket weavers.

THE NORTHWEST PACIFIC COAST - This area covers the coast of California, Oregon, Washington and parts of Canada. The Indians lived in wooden long houses in large villages. They fished the Pacific Ocean and hunted mountain sheep and goats.

Tribal Map & Word Find

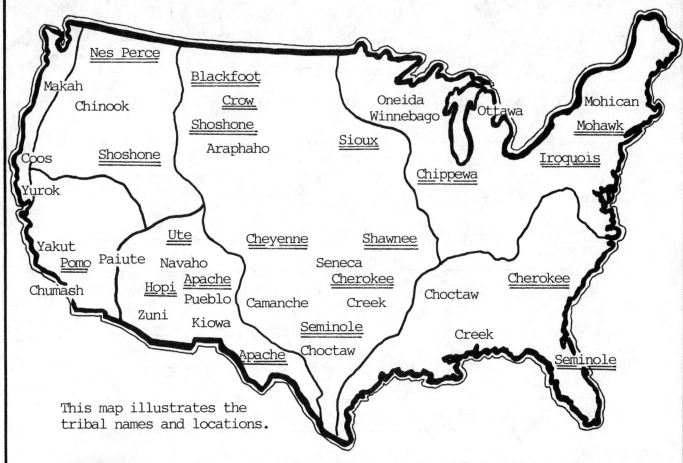

Nes Perce

Makah
Chinook

Blackfoot
Crow
Shoshone
Araphaho

Coos
Shoshone

Yurok

Oneida
Winnebago
Ottawa

Mohican
Mohawk

Sioux

Iroquois

Chippewa

Yakut
Pomo
Paiute
Ute
Navaho
Apache
Pueblo
Zuni
Kiowa

Cheyenne
Shawnee
Seneca
Cherokee
Creek
Choctaw

Cherokee

Chumash
Hopi

Camanche

Seminole
Choctaw

Creek

Seminole

Apache

This map illustrates the
tribal names and locations.

FIND THE UNDERLINED TRIBES IN THE PUZZLE BELOW.

ACTIVITY 6

```
Z X C F T C H E Y E N N E U K L P O I M J U
S D F G H J K L O L M N B H V C D F G H Y J
I S E T G H C H I P P E W A U K L P O M N B
O W D C V B N M J H T S X S E M I N O L E P
U S E R S E T Y U U T E Z X C V F G H B N M
X Z S W H Q W E R T Y U I O P A P A C H E Y
P O M O O D F G Y T R F V B N M K J H N M M
W T Y H S S F G H J K I O L B T Y H S A Q W
F S E F H F G T M O H A W K L X C S X Z A S
S X C V O G B T Q F G B N M A E R T F D C C
H D F T N C H E R O K E E E C F V B S M T R
O W C V E Z W C R V T B Y N K M I D H F R O
P I R O Q U O I S C V B G F F D R T A H F W
I S W E C V R T B N J U M K O O D R W H Y U
S D F R N E S P E R C E H Y O N J V N T Y H
Z X E W Q T Y U I O I O P L T S Y U E O K L
M S A W E C V T B N H G F D S A W Q E U P O
```

Research Page

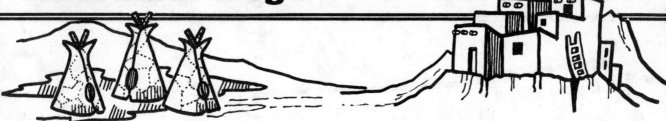

1. Write the name of the American Indian tribe you have chosen here.

    _____

2. Where did the tribe live? _____

3. What type of homes did they have? _____

4. What types of crafts did they make? _____

    _____

5. What foods did they eat? _____

    _____

6. What type of life did they live? _____

    _____

    _____

    _____

7. Name a famous person from this tribe. _____

8. What is important about this person? _____

    _____

    _____

    _____

9. What do you like most about this tribe? _____

    _____

    _____

    _____

    _____

10. On a separate piece of paper draw a picture of a member of the tribe
    in native costume or a picture of their Indian village.

Creative Writing

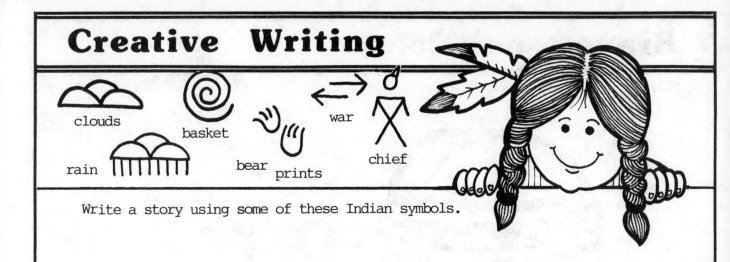

clouds

basket

war

rain

bear prints

chief

Write a story using some of these Indian symbols.

tepee

hill

running water

hunt

summer

friends

bird

food

deer

Brave and Canoe

Make copies of the Indian brave and canoe onto brown construction paper. Color and cut out.

Fold the canoe along the dotted line and punch holes where indicated. Stich together with yarn.

Cut out the oar and glue to the Indian brave's hands. Place him in the canoe.

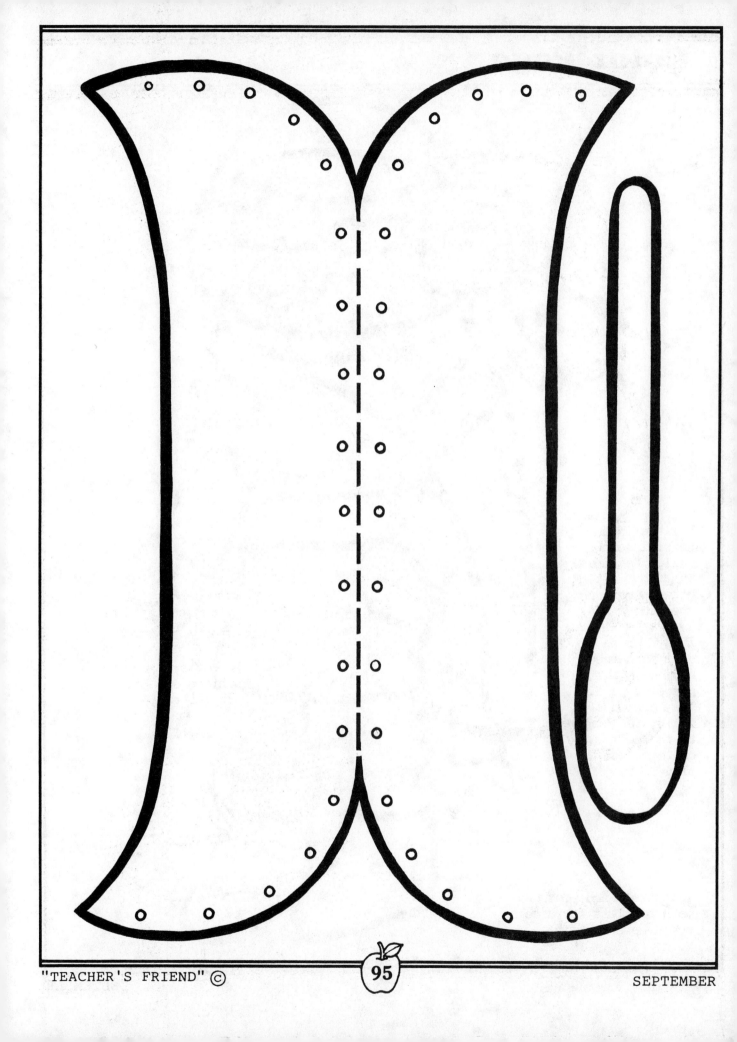

The Hopi Indians believe in super-natural beings called Kachinas. They form a link between man and the gods.

This Kachina doll is carved from one flat piece of wood. The Kachina dolls are given to the Hopi children as play toys.

Teachers: Add your own math problems for a color by numbers activity.

Bulletin Boards and more!

27 FLAVORS

Jimmy | Cathy
Mary Ann | Jeff
Fred | Pattie
Wayne | Toni

ICE CREAM FLAVORS

Let this giant ice cream cone welcome your students to class.

Enlarge the cone onto poster board and use year after year.

You might even like to make ice cream name tags for each student. An afternoon ice cream treat could also be a special back to school surprise.

COLORFUL HELPERS

This colorful idea will help keep track of classroom helpers.

Make crayon boxes from folded sheets of construction paper. Cut crayons from colored paper, also. Label with the children's names. Insert the crayons into the appropriate box.

WELCOME ABOARD!

Welcome your students to class with this nautical theme.

Cut the sails from white butcher paper and the hull from blue. Print student names on the sails with felt pens.

Later in the day read a sea story to the class.

and more...

CALENDAR BULLETIN BOARD

This year-round board changes each month and encourages your students to do creative things.

Select a board that is large enough to accommodate all the days of the month. You might wish to cut construction paper into 8" squares and pin to the board. Add numbers that can be changed monthly.

Pin to the calendar anything you wish—an A+ paper, a holiday symbol, a birthday card, student awards, etc.

CLASS HELPER TREE

A bare tree on your bulletin board can provide a handy way to display student helpers.

Cut a large tree from brown butcher paper and pin to the board. Students can cut leaves from construction paper, adding their names with felt markers. Label the branches of the tree with classroom jobs. Add student leaves to the appropriate branches.

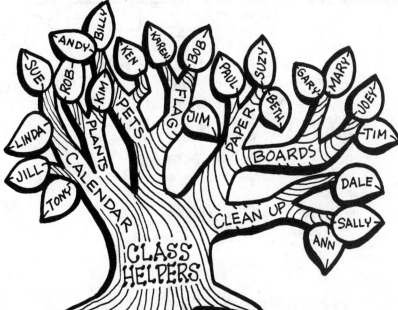

SIGN IN BULLETIN BOARD

Cover a classroom bulletin board with colored butcher paper. Add the words "WELCOME BACK" to the board.

Using water based felt-tipped pens, ask students to sign in when they arrive.

(Do not use permanent markers as they might bleed through the paper and onto the board.)

and more...

REMEMBER....

Enlarge this hand on poster board and display on the class bulletin board. Tie a piece of yarn to the extended finger.

List your classroom rules at the side of the board. This will serve as a great visual reminder throughout the year.

REMEMBER...
THESE RULES

1. Stay in your seat.

2. Raise your hand to speak.

3. Don't talk to your neighbor.

CLASS CHAMPS

Enlarge this super heavyweight onto poster board and display on a bulletin board.

Pin student names around the board or class writing assignments.

This is a great motivator for good work!

KINDER"GARDEN"

What a great way to welcome your little ones to class the first day! Have large cut paper flowers displayed on the class bulletin board. After the children have settled down for the day, pass out small paper plates. Ask the children to color a picture of themselves in the center of their plate. Label each plate with the child's name. Pin each plate to the center of each flower.

Welcome to Kinder"garden"

Andy   Tim   Kim   Susy
Tom   Joey   Ann   Jim

and more...

HAPPY BIRTHDAY

Make twelve construction paper pockets and label with the name of each month of the year. Pin them along the bottom of the class bulletin board. Write student names and birth dates on index cards or strips of paper. Store them in the appropriate pockets. As each month approaches, display the birthday cards associated with that month.

CAN YOU TIE YOUR SHOES?

Use this cute worm to motivate children to learn to tie their own shoes. Label a green paper plate with the name of each student. Draw a funny worm face to one plate and attach a bow tie and pipe cleaner antennae. As the children learn to tie their shoes, attach a pair of paper boots to the bottom of their paper plate. Soon your class worm will become a centipede.

THE BIRTHDAY TRAIN

Have your entire class jump aboard the "Birthday Train." Half sheets of construction paper can serve as the train's cars. Cut round circles for the wheels. Label each car with the months of the year. Display children's pictures or names in the appropriate cars.

and more...

MEET THE SCHOOL STAFF

The office bulletin board can be used to recognize the members of your staff. Take snapshots of all school personnel and mount each picture on the board with title and name.

This is a terrific way to welcome new students and their parents.

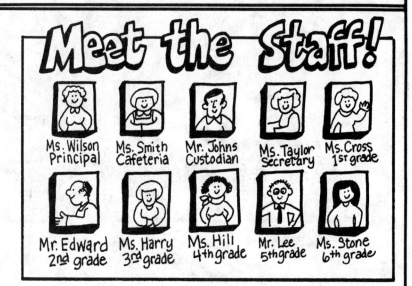

LESSON LINE UP

Make dresses, shirts and pants from cut paper, fabric, or wallpaper samples. With a marker, write the names of subjects to be studied in school. (You might like to add real lace and buttons to your creations.)

Stretch a piece of twine or yarn across a bulletin board and hang the clothes with real clothespins.

WISE OWLS

Paper bag owl puppets can be used to welcome students to school. Have each student make their own puppet and display it on the bulletin board. A paper cut tree branch and leaves should already be in place. Label each owl with the child's first name.

Laughing Books

Create a great library bulletin board by simply enlarging these "Laughing Books" on poster board and displaying them in the classroom.

Enlarge this character to bulletin board size and create a "Super Student" display.

Each month you can change the character with a few minor adjustments. For September, place a cut paper apple in one hand and a lunch box in the other. In October, add a jack o' lantern, Halloween mask and trick or treat bag. For December, dress him in a white cotton beard and red paper cap.

Super Student

Your students will be anxious to learn what new costume you have created each month.

Birthdays

Cut 12 cupcakes from construction paper or poster board. Label the frosting with the name of each month. List student birthdays below, as shown. Place a cut paper candle on the current birthday cupcake.

MARCH
ANN 3rd
SAM 14th

APRIL
MIKE 19th
JOEY 21st

Label one candle per student. Each month display candles on a class birthday cake.

Use patterns to enlarge to bulletin board size.

happy birthday

Helpers

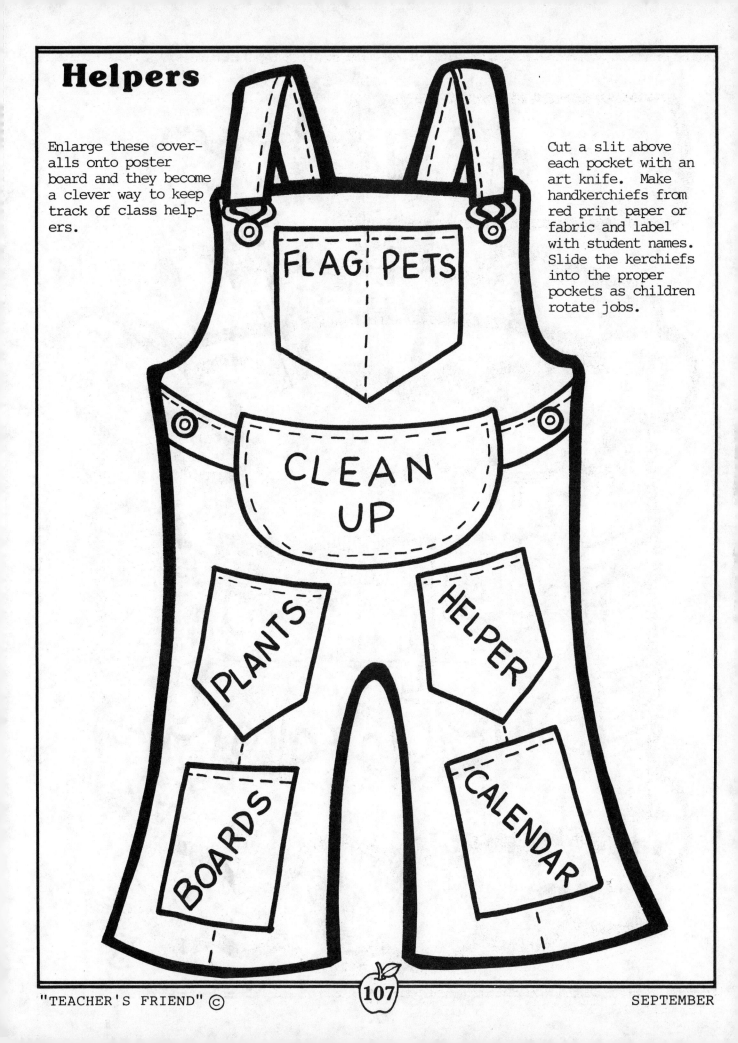

Enlarge these cover-alls onto poster board and they become a clever way to keep track of class helpers.

Cut a slit above each pocket with an art knife. Make handkerchiefs from red print paper or fabric and label with student names. Slide the kerchiefs into the proper pockets as children rotate jobs.

FLAG · PETS

CLEAN UP

PLANTS

HELPER

BOARDS

CALENDAR

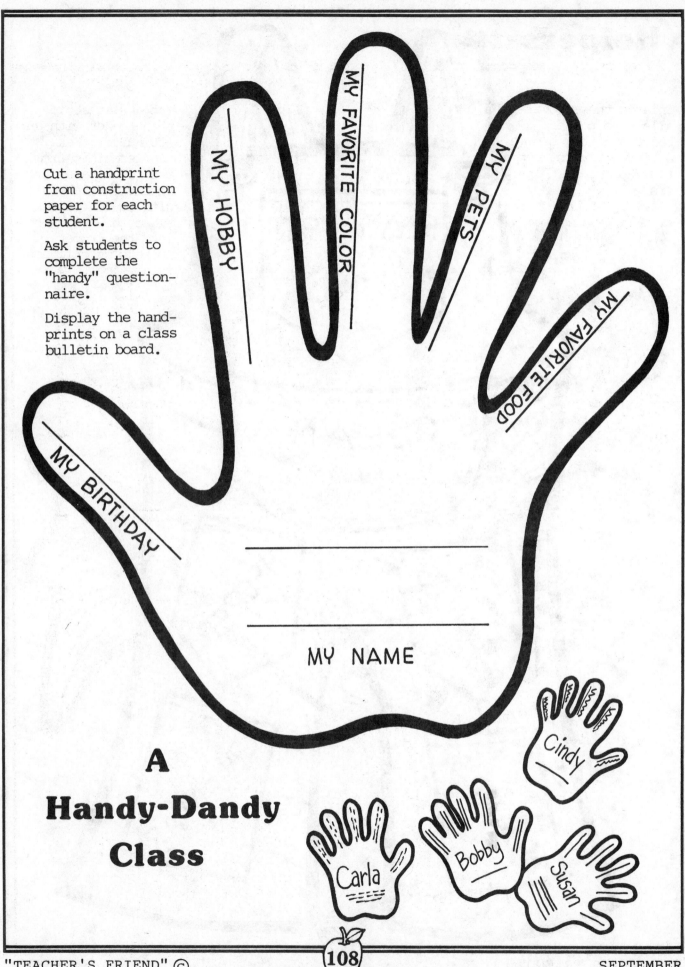

Cut a handprint from construction paper for each student.

Ask students to complete the "handy" questionnaire.

Display the handprints on a class bulletin board.

MY HOBBY

MY FAVORITE COLOR

MY PETS

MY FAVORITE FOOD

MY BIRTHDAY

MY NAME

A Handy-Dandy Class

Cindy

Carla

Bobby

Susan

Tree Pattern

Attach leaves to the tree with straight pins. Turn one leaf over each day—that person becomes the class helper for the day.

Snowflakes, flowers, birds, butterflies and hearts can be added as the seasons change.

BARE TREE PATTERN

Enlarge this bare tree pattern onto brown butcher paper and pin it to a class bulletin board. Have students cut fall leaves from colored construction paper. Ask them to write their names on the back of each leaf.

Answer Key

ACTIVITY 1

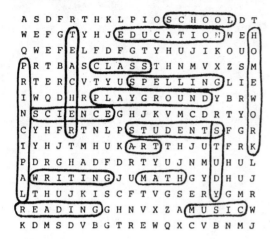

```
A S D F R T H K L P I O (S C H O O L) D T
W E F G T Y H J (E D U C A T I O N) W E H
Q W E F E L F D F G T Y H U J I K O U O
(P) R T B A S (C L A S S) T H N M V X Z S M
R T E R C V T Y U (S P E L L I N G) L I E
I W Q D H R (P L A Y G R O U N D) Y B R W
N (S C I E N C E) G H J K V M C D R T Y O
C Y H F (R) T N L P (S T U D E N T S) F G R
I Y H J T M H U K (A R T) T H J U T F R K
P D R G H A D F D R T Y U J N M U H U L
A (W R I T I N G) J U (M A T H) G Y D H U J
L T H U J K I S C F T V G S E R Y G M R
(R E A D I N G) G H N V X Z A (M U S I C) W
K D M S D V B G T R E W Q X C V B N M J
```

ACTIVITY 2

ANSWER THESE TRUE AND FALSE QUESTIONS ABOUT JOHNNY APPLESEED.

T (F) Johnny Appleseed was born in the state of Ohio.

(T) F Johnny Appleseed's real name was John Chapman.

T (F) Johnny Appleseed was given his nickname because he loved to eat apples.

T (F) Johnny Appleseed did not like the Indians.

(T) F Johnny Appleseed was a real man.

ACTIVITY 3

United States of America

MEXICO

Pacific Ocean

Gulf of Mexico

Belize

Guatemala

ACTIVITY 4

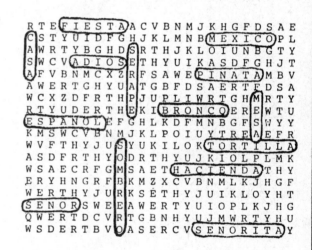

```
R T E (F I E S T A) A C V B N M J K H G F D S A E
(C) S T Y U I D F G H J K L M N B (M E X I C O) P L
A W R T Y B G H D (S) R T H J K L O I U N B G T Y
S W C V (A D I O S) E T H Y U I K A S D F G H J T
A F V B N M C X Z R F S A W E (P I N A T A) M B V
W C X Z D F R T H P J U P L I W R T G H M R T Y
R T Y U D E R T H E K I (B R O N C O) E R E W T U
(E S P A N O L) E F G H L K D F M N B G F S W Y Y
K M S W C V B N M J K L P O I U Y T R E A E F R
W V F T H Y J U S Y U K I L O K (T O R T I L L A)
A S D F R T H Y O D R T H Y U J K I O L P L M K
W S A E C R F G M S A E T (H A C I E N D A) T H Y
E R Y H N G R F B K M Z X C V B N M L K J H G F
W E R T H Y J U R K S E T H Y J U I K L O Y H T
(S E N O R) S W E E A W E R T Y U I O P L K J H G
Q W E R T D C V R T G B N H Y U J M W R T Y H U
W S D E R T B V O A S E R C V (S E N O R I T A) Y
```

ACTIVITY 5

MATCH THESE FACTS ABOUT MEXICO.

MEXICO'S NEIGHBOR TO THE NORTH

MEXICAN INDEPENDENCE DAY

THE CAPITAL OF MEXICO

THE LANGUAGE OF THE MEXICAN PEOPLE

THEY BUILT THE MEXICAN PYRAMIDS

CINCO DE MAYO

THE COLORS OF THE MEXICAN FLAG

THE PRIEST WHO SPOKE AGAINST SPAIN

THE AZTECS

THE 5th OF MAY

RED, GREEN AND WHITE

UNITED STATES OF AMERICA

MEXICO CITY

SEPTEMBER 16th

FATHER HILDALGO

SPANISH

ACTIVITY 6

FIND THE UNDERLINED TRIBES IN THE PUZZLE BELOW.

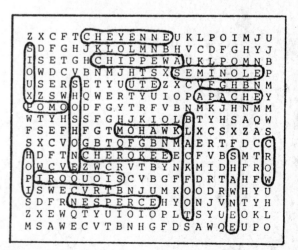

```
Z X C F T (C H E Y E N N E) U K L P O I M J U
S D F G H J (K L O L M N B) H V C D F G H Y J
I S E T G H (C H I P P E W A) U K L P O M N B
O W D C V B N M J H T S X (S E M I N O L E) P
U S E R (S) E T Y U (U T E) Z X C V F G H B N M
X Z S W H Q W E R T Y U I O P (A P A C H E) Y
P O M O O D F G Y T R F V B N M K J H N M M
W T Y H S S F G H J K I O L B T Y H S A Q W
F S E F H F G T M O H A W K L X C S X Z A S
S X C V O G B T Q F G B N M A E R T F D C C
H D F T N (C H E R O K E E) C F V B S M T R
O W C V E Z W C R V T B Y N K M I D H F R O
P I R O Q U O I S C V B G F F D R T A H F W
I S W E C V R T B N J U M K O O D R W H Y U
S D F R (N E S P E R C E) H Y O N J V N T Y H
Z X E W Q T Y U I O I O P L T S Y U E O K L
M S A W E C V T B N H G F D S A W Q E U P O
```